aeromancy garage

KEN TAYLOR

DOS MADRES

2020

DOS MADRES PRESS INC.
P.O. Box 294, Loveland, Ohio 45140
www.dosmadres.com   editor@dosmadres.com

Dos Madres is dedicated to the belief that the small press is essential to the vitality of contemporary literature as a carrier of the new voice, as well as the older, sometimes forgotten voices of the past. And in an ever more virtual world, to the creation of fine books pleasing to the eye and hand.

Dos Madres is named in honor of Vera Murphy and Libbie Hughes, the "Dos Madres" whose contributions have made this press possible.

Dos Madres Press, Inc. is an Ohio Not For Profit Corporation and a 501 (c) (3) qualified public charity. Contributions are tax deductible.

Executive Editor: Robert J. Murphy

Illustration & Book Design: Elizabeth H. Murphy
www.illusionstudios.net
Cover photo: *blue laws* by Ken Taylor © 2018. Used by permission of the North Carolina Museum of Art.

Typeset in Adobe Garamond Pro & Skia
ISBN 978-1-953252-15-9
Library of Congress Control Number: 2020949086

for Nate

CONTENTS

Strange the surprise in that sky
where unwillingly footfalls turn
and voices swell in its pregnant center.
An obscure meadow goes by.

José Lezama Lima

translated by Nathaniel Tarn

stratus

cloud in the shape of jazz hands

worship by relative deprivation is tiny spirit-finger animation
without a toy inside

      slant show & choir disruption of other objects of taste

a tacit ploy falsely applied exceeding all rigor to grow pink &
white   splashed with dread

      webbing for the last of waste   in bed with a nod to
splay   is how trigger-happy thinks

this impure act of now past all sensible image razzle dazzles the
low & curdled cream   grinning in a blackface tradition

& inelastic dreams work a tight gauge & craft submissive fabric
with lace at the cuff   in full favor of scoring

      hollow practice tests the hold of balance
& lapping claims no division or decrease

but when the paper mill stops clapping arrests will follow

cloud in the shape of a mall walker

bound to a wearable the flâneur knows ellipsoidal to be the course around a body a field of two million bricks & parquetry the gristle on foot guided by an interface synched to sky to be happy from the perimeter in the body is a scene suspended from thread knitting impulse to concrete where absence means something his animus his seeming just short of sadness everything designed to be shallow the best sacerdotal thing he says no to new updates adding buzz escalates in the anchor store thinking the heart is a beaten gap between assumed & true facing toast points as a lure to fleece free tea a way of tethering shirts of his youth placed & priced not to fit the body is a ratio of solid to void flensing v. feedbag five laps to the cookie he checks his wrist to find heat he won't spend coveting the circumbendibus stroll of the rental cop roaming would be crime scenes his badge adrift in imaginings beyond the uniform mouthing the talk of coroners decoding blood & patterns void of blood skin shrinkage wound study hilt imprints ligature marks leaving trace the part of the body where prints can be found is not always the best place to lift them

a model staging more carrot than stick leads a perfect horse past perfect shoes reduced to a sum no one can pay he catches her eye over glaze swirling backward on red velvet the color scheme of half his age implying rose when blue runs out like her gaze does withdrawing from antique fuzz he needs a stunt utility or mindset fixed on the scale of what a self really is mixing the figure & abstraction seeking fitness in a copy of foraging thinks a person real or made-up is screening flaws of framework heartened by circuitry he samples pulse upping

rigor to fast casual taking big out of the box to put fresh in
it deems himself an avatar a thing standing in for a kind of
star an aggravated body unwinding in free-fall spun like an
airplane or amusement park death a cartoon swiping glister
from breath shy of anvils rising confessing ruin in alcoves
among the fair immune to mercy & tides

cloud in the shape of hedging

> *the larger the dada the bigger the hole*
>
> Jack Spicer

we came of age in black hats & gluten-free cages
to fund flat-footed rocketry aimed at some appliance
never caught up with during wingtip days

the reverse cowgirl saddles the *universal circus*
& is first to pitch straddling as better spurring
by elevating click-thrus from crack spread to money shot

a longer measure of downstairs is covering a short position
to avoid debriding by swapping headcount from the sales side
as extra coverage against decay

soft purchase lights up the electorate with forecast
nomenclature to trick out the uptick of fool's wheat
with deflationary glancing

their margin call misses ball dancing again
please pass the illiquid future of exurbia lousy with topiary
while traffic panders lucite in a single file of tombstones

cloud in the shape of sun ra

how brave of the moth straight into the grill floodlit victim
in search of praise i'm not bug-hunting with a taste for spilled
blood packing ethereal jars hoping to add pattern to collection
i'm keeping wheels between reflections & listening to him long
down can't tell what vapors are up if there's moon stew dancing
thru pews haggling with people of earth & fellow travelers of
the empty foxhole behind the sideman beside himself out in
front of water recycling the thing there's always another thing
in a cosmos as big as this dotted by samples held at the spine
fixed wings will not deliver chance will defect to mid-fidelity
ending a return to the most evil place brotherly love egyptian
system cut with alabama gatefold sleeve 180-gram vinyl means
a thicker record of the back roads struck by high-beams striking
a row of diamonds the interstellar meeting ground for god's
appointment

cloud in the shape of flossing

authorities say the entry to your face is foul   poor
potty mouth   & a far cry from the ply of powder
agents rehearsing new eyeteeth   lacking oversight in
coining loss to put fondant where your toothpaste is

dark matter is key to hygiene patterns   the gums should
be trained in concealing what a gate lets in   everything
decays to the next level of correction under unsupervised
conditions

authorities say spend extra minutes & believe that something
you can't see is darning a rupture next to natural teeth
the root of fleece or tuft of wool for spinning yarns in contrary
rending

announcing the residue of the king's food for his retinue is a
bunch to say around impairment & requires post-incident silk
sawing hollows & hills   plaque is not detached only the
reference is removed

authorities say whip out lots of inches in tribute to the fair
                    while deleting porn with waxed expectation
                              nylon curving in slender interproximal
care thru slots between those that almost touch

in a periodontal version of schrödinger's cat   using
teeth to gage trust   the producers stack the studies treating
flock control by flopping physics in the clinical hustle of super
aromatic positioning

authorities say take up dirty string to find hurt in a series of
figure eights   it's normal to feel ache in dislodging
hypothesized arcana   better to infer this so the
standard model works

two finger discounts leave deposits in your calculus account
  toothsome reckoning for selling the stink of down
river mouth   spoiling filigree to push mint by
whispering a quotable rhyme lifting market share

cloud in the shape of the way
the mind in a dream state recombines

after Paul Klee

light learned on a rooftop
       savors translucency
            measures flow thru ochre

before arriving at unease
as bitumen or smoke

the shift of gears quickening
asserts the sound of futures in other frames

lawn
stirred sky
early burst of a star

desiring beyond figuring traces two & one
in fractional parts of a sphere
& pinpoints an exhausted balloon

something of breath soon flattens distinctions
between arrows below the threshold of sculpture
& the only door   closed to a call to prayer

cloud in the shape of spelling the alphabet

glance in your journey menu to the in-betweens
thru eyes calibrated for stigmata
    & attempt a graver theory of why some are thought to
    belong to the bow
& others brittle willows that tack more letters on

sex is not the loop of census taking
& gender clusters near a soup of surrender
risking synergy or a tumble off the safe candy list
drawn to the arrow of sometimes there is queer so quickly

mapped in fear
the so-called stump speech with a ramp device
    is the press of notes
        is dormie all at once
& an inner ghost chasing stops pulled out by alto sax
orthography rolling twenty on the stimp

inner prestidigitator
inner pickpocket outside doing time
old hand at springing key signatures
with fingering supersaturated sugar
    virgin beauty as gettable song
prone to sneaky long inside the leather

the no-good cookie session tracks soothing
beside a range of ugly things said
in defense of the regular way to collapse silence
or in divides contending for incoherent splendor

biology gets murky due to genital sensations
difference meets fixed not budging
stymying a nuanced style of bulging expectations
        of doubling up on sameness
not all cruelties are correct

this alterity quiets then startles & reaches for a fetishistic
hue beyond the grayscales of closed-circuit
        for the tower of mommy not there
derma playing out as gunfire on a hurt surface

liminal bottling at the source
mixes with current strands
& exits to exist as dance
            as text clear of an anthologizing stance
                as headdress
                    as piercing
                        as trembling
arriving
to play no less striking than dear

cloud in the shape of a cold case

it's not going to end well for bob i know this after bariolage by
strings you meet someone in a b-film it's sure to come back day
for night blue on a close up of pretend his foe slinks around
glitter off the motor lodge deep end cast as edgy based on real
life drama & while i don't know the instrument i can guess
the style of blunt trauma or the proxy that radio is safe for the
good guy for the hero patter no cleavage in radio born from
scraping up glendale rent or hunting an epoxy to cure vaporized
served as prime the pig-tailed fräulein can be conjured from
sputum in back of the mouth instead of smearing until he
finally chews scenery at the window losing more with smaller
plates of dinner theatre the crane shot fades to a skewed frame
that plucks heartless which brings me to the part set behind a
sliding barrier to entry admitting spatter but not woe

hogan i know nothing nothing

cloud in the shape of the shipping forecast

slight or moderate becoming moderate or rough

> his better half bends but doesn't block the sun too close
> to burr grinding speech not far from storming over
> squares of sea she hides her eyes in razor wire winks
> against the low current & their breach tamped down

moderate or rough occasionally very rough later

> her finger sings on the lip of air opening against a span
> pierced by windows & asks about his time away but his
> time away is still ticking he replays cheering he wasn't
> invited to instead of feigning not to hear

very rough or high becoming very high for a time

> if the ferry comes soon he'll get alone time with the
> medicine ball her map interrogates him with bays &
> straights no longer there his feet find heartwood pine
> once stacked to acclimatize before roses changed scale

cyclonic or thundery increasing to gale perhaps severe gale

> they went out to smoke & heard fluting he quit
> requesting burn permits to set the distance on fire she
> pledged desire flooding to guests they sank to something
> short of happy giving porch chairs away too soon

good becoming moderate or poor

he slinks in a serpent suit on the cornice of the
proud & seeks the precession of equinoxes she
stirs from a spell telling time by bells & now loves
another after he cut her out of a car conjures sails
in her ceiling

slight or moderate occasionally rough showers then fair

cloud in the shape of the goths

the film in question is a counting animal with lines applied
in scorn sloping starboard & viewed more times due to a
click-bait ornament it tries to wipe the link between those
that dreamed of the gayest hardcore punk & a mini-lesson of
mortuary scaring peasants to church your drop-down is a gaze
on the lower danube lingering in the chill of baptismal water
if only out of respect for the dead the new need despoilers to
spread the weight of tall walls matching savagery with kissing
their banners lifting damp & reducing sperm count please
remember to use blood as an accent color to boost announcing
in your mirror why raise a rain-gutter when you can create a
monster the bondage pants of debutantes may devise a buttress
to sorrow but any backwoods thinker struggles to solve medieval
problems like balloon folding in the sense that bela lugosi's gone
striving to be exact in a manner that has soured knowing the
vaulted ceiling is a workhorse in corpse paint referring to pale
complexity your vampire singing may be stuck on horizontal
but is crucial to the return of black gloss in the trailer park
threnody exposed with a slow shutter truth beholding the plot
behind clerestory math the armature of piped masonry edging
the release of light

cloud in the shape of adjustment

her trunk application is electric twitch in a wet blanket during
a dry rendition of dean martin's bad ice that serves as preamble
to the raided premises feeling

if running shoes stand in the sun they're cheaper on-line

she says over the client face down on examination paper
coveting the edition of what's covering his feet

his mind is rotating tires

hers is cracking sudoku

he dreams of drugstore brittle passed off as homemade among
potlucks between rock-a-billy sets driving dulcet innuendo

she ponders limerence while reading the stiffened state thru
the lens of reminisced charts where misalignment found by
touching invites a slower breath & his head turning sharply

later she digs two-digits deep into the calendar

his eyes release down the road not taken

they swap damage in the banter of co-pay before he sounds
the bell that signals an exit or entrance

cloud in the shape of an air gap

is ducking the X for Y format   & use of nonce words
what's said means tagging its reverse   in perfect forward
secrecy   foisted for better   the trees are seed cabinets
grass hostility beneath the flower process   doing the work
of pillage   edit   erase   in the pad crashed for keys   to
decipher a splotch of lilac   thrown away by memory   love
is turned on bliss   in clean cascades   not paranoid enough
citizen   the smallest of grace notes   & a string of friends
marking themselves safe in wreckage

the shortest route home has been found take providence

there comes a time when attribution dressed in pansy is the
value   a field of heartsease   between those that joined
exploiting & others beyond ride-sharing   black boxes don't
tally attrition like the allure behind curtain auroras   bromides
steal melody from a long-limbed tune & speak of buzz cut
days   frozen in wavy borders   diving under falling stars &
bars for glory   means lost early   satellites fondle private
space by way of achievement badges   ribbons   breaking
points   to track every hued breath

those that bought the turn of the screw also bought the dead

behind spook-speak runs tough episodes   plainclothes not
always a cloak   logging keystrokes as salted truths to be harder
to hack   exposing a target with hay-colored hair   using cash
is still traceable   the fenced-in portion not taking backtalk
ticking red next to freedom of intrusion   rapid eye is just more
clock syphoning flash drives   & a festschrift for three letter
agency   bite down on popcorn time   & hug a cushion to
your chest   as hush-hush streams by   the false promise
of anodyne

cloud in the shape of a praise poem

cuts from every wild rose chasing creeley skipping out on the
run sparking others in the idea of flight

this goddamned barred rock hand-picked with one good eye
drew on a feral line & slipped enjambment in a break for honey
too low to suckle

*first you wonder if they're separate plots but no form is never more
than* blinkered embracing husbandry

fuck you for raising these fowl i love you though i won't re-coop
the flock spoofing *hen of the woods*   so said dance of the bur
oak savannah

the pliant roost under firefly wink & cluck their caveats among
a host that would devour   accruing to who blinks first

cloud in the shape of a portrait of the artist as a shadow of his former self

after Kerry James Marshall

the document projects egged effacement through an aperture
of grinning   as gap-toothed absorbing   interiors echo
absence in a series representing scenes   one-drop composes
the placement of bone around a telling smile   & sardonic
comingling   of comedy not laughable in the classical
sense   mirth in the house as comity   reciting heart of the
art of nightfall that beats out an improvised study of *perfect
practice makes perfect*   play practice makes striking stunning
crafting a comely life that tastes like church

sunday-go-to-meeting clothes wrap the city of big shoulders
of figures that can't be seen as real   three-fifths in tune with
twoness in a hat tipped to cheshire   hep-cat ungrasped from
hepatic background   though buttoned-up by invisible   by
fragments from a boutonniereless conversation   parsing
lamentation that haunts museums   burning at both ends
abrades carbon with brilliance   depicting a rehearsal of
selves in the pose of a canary that swallows taste-making   &
is first responder to toxic

vanquishing a vanishing act with factually black magic   with
broken rosaries pushing against legacy with paint   rope-a-
dope rooted in tripping up tropes   exhausting refusal by
wearing it thin   curatorial plan to make haptic light flourish
in facture   to make looking seeing   pastimes inside the
kitchen rise thru the spectacle of scrapbook liturgy   *never
saw a picture not worth cutting out*   when a kind of kitsch
meets a slighted factor with pinkies up arranged as fleeing
thru a field the circles of mowing missed

this plinth above cornerstones is blankness fed by
methodical returning to formal refrains   to found the
collective filled with aspects not formerly there   reproofing
sweep of prior kith & ken by pigment as a coloring matter
turned splendid orison   more laminar than orpiment
more appaloosa than pinto   *moonlight* greater than *thor*
mars shortened by omission grounds ornamental   as a
joycean cut   marks presence inside previous reviewing
restored beauty denoting measure as *counter-archive*

cloud in the shape of crossing
        the face of a sundial

fast drawn
            & shot in the back of her argument
for alehouse clientele
at arm's-length from armless sculpture
rehearsing blushes inside a vellum stockade

i finger past integuments
seeking   *dates   wool   meats   grain*
over contours below a chanticleer splendor
or sulfuric coverlet born of seafoam

she becomes the figure that swoons for all things blooming
in centripetal twine
divining smolder in retrograde
her melody above the musk of her myrtle crown
declares love a paired idea
            with pushbacks
a shakedown admitting neon by impulsive frisk
a nude feast for ishtar

her cunning stalks rapture
played out in suits of wands
dealt from a lower risk position
the straight-line approach in forever curving
            as sweetmeat transiting
or slurred tremolos for lucifer

each animation is a host of trios
          kinesis fooling gnosis
like owl eyes on moth wings
no lamping in the emphasis area
perched on the porch of her ear
where rain melts lead

she calls to the shade-grown
          to wind-swept plants
counts lesser lights in the hour of misgiving
beyond fire-quenching
          beyond cavity & chaos
& shows no witness marks
          no signs of footing further off
but strands coiling from the smoking gun
of morning becoming

                                        for Phoebe

cloud in the shape of little friday

luck by the book
is carny fog in bright reminiscence
after a break from paperback eyes

the near-fine chorister
shelves the ruins of supper
blesses kindling in no wind

jumpstarts trouser jazz
with a foxed frontispiece
in the margin of the stacks

winter wheeling tracks fleet movement
like a spent nymph struggling
on a dark surface above diesel geese

hanging doors open to regular lapsing
        light reading nipping nothing in the bud
bookmarked to a sawed-off barrel fire

dubbing thursday to let whiskey in early

cloud in the shape of misunderstanding haiku

this swoops like a hurried
neck tattoo   returning to the pump handle
passing off sunk costs   deeper

than birds   in more clawed
helpings than knitting feet   even pocket pool
won't cure a parting with

mora   going up & down
in seventeen gears   founding seasons in pairs
falling in with syllabic mishap

syllabic misconstrue   strummed   plucked   cut
as an askance grab   as western faux
pas casting in eastern deeps

& not fishing further out
by not catching the gist of imagist
in capital waves of pumice

it may take the appeal
of pipe cleaner people accepting only cash
to put hands on property

when pickup mud flaps say
prelapsarian never looked so good   long after
depicting moons to capture time

adjective plus noun of noun

& surrealistic pillow talks to summon blossoms
bayans chopsticks   or costume brooches

piecework sweat of mercy
ever situated in quiddity along a bitter
path   ensnares flow by rooting

soil from being spirited away
        & the part which *does* the verb
like flicks of silk dewdrops

of sleep is lamp-black carbon
as seen on TV   shall i spank
you with a heat map

& drape tickertape about your
small shoulders as heroic lack of agency
lit by sake   or will

bowers lousy with mimesis announce
surplus in the waft of state breezes
& ripening plums   or can

chenille respired across damp *sencha*
        past supply curves like open sutures aping
the rigor of overcoming hurt

opaque poetry is mostly frowned
upon   like coming early   cops upstage display
behind the syndrome of tall

poppies   asking with mouth organs
to read their lips   attempting *moshi moshi*
but saying *topsy-turvy*   expecting order

from unschooled fish   can we
not aim to be exact & make
boo-boo part of the refrain

& chart labor in small
lights   in a quick-change caper over pickets
in linguistic & terpsichorean economies

caning canary torts   green peaches
& polka dots folded in a chifforobe
of uncertain origins beyond practice

urge a laundry stamp aesthetic
in whirr & sashay without limiting conditions
or thinking up blind alleys

tell the truth   *but first*
a lil' chi-chi   is bloodletting in nonchalance
when counting weights on fingers

as eros arises a rose
remains   *& is as if a palimpsest*
adding sacrifice to one-breath recitation

cloud in the shape of a song for jesus
in three-quarter time

elders said scripture said

                                         god

on the second line streets
by the shortest & unmeasured
just this side of apologue

                                         is hard

the best appendage to emerge uncontested
longing to remember nowhere sorting now

do you claim three & four is there
& gone against the beat
        call & recall
& not those who suspend

                                         believing

imploring a nimbus
thru lattices of litanies
struggling for sense

dear your face here
                speaking in red
                behind shutters
                teach me how you come in
                how you go

if i restage off-harmony to when i could pray
to el   al   elohim   allah   to buddha   to you

among these roundelays asking for treasure
       extra alabaster helpings
with frenzied breath
to unnamable listening
       does my ever-lifted reach

                 love

this dirge is a waltz
drawn in a key tough to heed
brass easing up to reed
       to a clemency machine
in praise by making

                 instead of
                 leaning on
                 the take

cloud in the shape of vodka

trust me you can dance
unfettered in tulips
   beyond swan & vapors
with ice in offset vacuum points inclined to ecliptic
certified on the furthest of limbs
& ruled by the shortest of lords

you must chance believing in the dose-response affinity
or find an alibi hunting a heads-up penny
& while it's true that bankers' hours are better than bakers'
hours   their notes don't pass the smell test

check your consonants at the door
& go all savannah on me
   small batching is fun like bending
   & subject to towing
if you ride the young potatoes in this chimerical plan
you'll find heaven patched with the flowing fabric of little
waters
   & slot drums'll become slit drums'll become
the wobbling fear of being cut up in pieces
or cooked with the eyes still in

hold your tongue & toe a straight line under a quarter moon
to a sign that tries to say *sale signs for sale soon*
   it's a way of speaking for trees with trunk support
& striving for the mill with twelve buckets in magnitudes
per square arc second

some say nothing endows the will
like the great cannonball rolling in
to change a bach chorale to *this here*

walk back your divination system
to the pet relief area
if you face east & i fret in no direction

who is holy

cloud in the shape of trying to act casual

plunking down for a spit-test kit is betting against popsicle
sticks in the kinfolk lampshade way or flunked chatter
warmed by unrestricted sweets

my plumb line is sailing in failed flowers
& forever chasing barcodes based on the hope
of a fetching silhouette

& the full picture of base pairs requires not seeing accident
in genes modeled on accretion & sequence
& the burying of fine print

to snuff out all sparks but one with pocking snow
or the opposite of sticking has a history
of stuffing ballots to prop up awkward logic

we sorted *hiding in the family tree*
by progressive rolls of dice built on rules
that ring risk with burning bodies organized in pools

to find how brushwork strays from handedness
when forebears dodged early ends by fleeing claws
& minding the laws of arriving

i was raised in a house with painted-on ears
& invited to peer no further than the gorgeous blocking
of our stock footage on display

i trained on trials & teaser balloons
striving to beat the platform that invests in value chains
around happy data

my according clad in repositioned corduroy met all
the conditions for a scryer but only glimpsed a future
where *a mutt is really something to be*

it's just saliva
but a rogue leaf in the tracing loop is a turn
from enacting dust that wants more blueblood & less crew list

more oceanic & less desert
more likely to bounce light than feature the smell
of asparagus in pee

i never learned the theory of copying is picking up
not putting down & standing on tiptoe to be anything
except less than a neighbor

while letters send layers ahead
as glint-finding or folds in generational flow
to practice sameness in a stranger way

cloud in the shape of burnt soup

while their trespass bloomed like hemlock spilt from a habit
with another name for fucking the profile of hearty boiled
unwatched a toxic split which loosened tongues after they
knew of lust steeped in riddles of the ancients & occasionally
medicinal which escaped the lovers the pendant cone & fabulous
name issued from toxic hearts the winged seeds of subdivisions
landed quavering in parts masked by chance they were fooled
by this scalding that can soothe & agreed to rendezvous at the
corner of cypress & hemlock to be freed by conceits of the
ancients clutching in the habit of lovers espousing any sunny
name to conceal decay that might break the code of treacle
honeyed instead of toxic performed by the vent of little petals
offering open legs to keep from falling out with the ancients or
failing all they'd make a swap of neighboring like the storied
swallowing hemlock before habit crushed the lovers

cloud in the shape of a hat on a bed

the system you return to is blood hostile to the big exit   to a
wildcard ending   advancing your coonass name   in a parlay
for finer   despite the fraying straw of your cypher said to
keep all from harm   marginal advice resisting certainty   part
of your charm   dispensed with a cloth over your shoulder
stirring a roux

& talk of a priest's last vestment off indoors   the crown of a
king on a tomb   just the ticket to hinder lice   chalked up to
eclipses   hot dice   or any affinity to the spread   your dead
appear like clockwork between breaths & blue feet   where
shame won't need a bump from the backroom to play the
same numbers   to rub rosaries down with a chided thumb
protecting your embrace of beauty   as if connected to the
valorized corona of moving pictures

a farmer out standing in his field

is busted balls   is ribbing by namesake   & one of many
flocks strayed from   the art of giving up the ghost is two
doors out   your rule for ever arriving   where the hall is lined
with unearthed chicory cans   crammed with tamped down
currency   to later pin to clotheslines   floating fusty green
in blue   until your eyes wind down to petals   & fire set to
what remains

this is not comeuppance   or a fall by desire   or a harbinger of
luck run out   this is lagniappe   in a gulf wind calling

in memory of Loren Farmer

36

cloud in the shape of gnosis

a plane flies into the head of henry grimes   declining right to
left   over the sixth surface of sky   fourth going back over
brackish   his silhouette is extramundane   & animates the
tap root of his mill   spiraling past limits of thrown   ever
spilling further elsewhere

> his grip claps mint into quilting   past billows   past the
> seven   to the fixed stars occluded by light   knowing
> fullness is a field   is a set of values assigned to every
> space in time

my mind's body's tight with his kaleidoscopic kinship   bass
upholding essence   in deadpan delivery   his pearl at full
gallop is four & five   is nine

> *& nine is supposed to be everything*

another plane flies into the head of henry grimes   canted
in raptness   his ear takes in without rupture   he anchors
iterations of uncharted   swerve   pivot   small clearances
& the wind behind see-through tracing ecstasy

> solfeggio frequencies chartered by early green   & the
> galaxy scratched in his lower bout   reaching deeper
> than turbulence   deeper than slumber   selves ever
> mounting as chorus effects   as counterweight to flurry
> in troubling numbness to excitation

the head of henry grimes receives another plane   stannic push
to land in patterns spaced for jersey   alien dome that can take
it   can absorb wingspan & turbine in the line of casting   in
synch with mythic lingering

> his tune obliging capsized souls   bobbing in elemental
> lack   beseeching thru un-brushed teeth   rising thru
> perforations   thru punctures   in a tonic interlace of
> the unbegotten refrain   vestments drop from telluric
> framing   & collect at his feet   ready to lift off   as
> notes unspool without portioning

from woodshed to the serpentine path of *whereto we speed*   &
set for transport thru manifold boundaries   where what was
parceled is made one again   he shuts the book on the body
before confounding ground control

> *can't somebody smile   can't somebody be a king*

on a higher plane above the head of henry grimes   jet trails
pierce azure   disband in tufted streaks   unobstructed by
inner walls   his denouement suspending   bracing   bridging
holding so much aloft

cirrus

cloud in the shape of jazz to come

got a fat lip for the early stand against puffery for holding out to deliver a trance struck by lightning in spontaneous plastic outside changes injection-molded breaths of cream-colored acrylic enact the ritual of repeating notes against the repetition of damage looping back against history by a reverse calendar savant that sees the future as an acquired taste getting out of hand when one approaches hand to mouth & moves past zugzwang by busting up encroachment busting out from less a penalty in some cases a prize in others not making ends meet without friction working with vitreous tone poems operating the elevation of angels in ivory & gold non-crystalline for more impact strength but behaving inelastically in a manner incompatible with section work this knotted up stricture will not stand in music issuing from the thigh of jupiter that loses the piano at first pressing by rejecting pre-written tablature of well-worn beauties in the way of pushing idioms past limits with squawks & honks extending technique by wavering on purpose while arriving on waves from atlantic untethering abrasions & breezes by slurring mournful in a balladeering smoke compact floes voicing the throat raising spherical heat in roomy production blue fugues of an apothecary geisha listening on the party line to another voluptuary tale submitting to ice cream truck licks overstepping the edge device of tumbleweeds phrasing the thru-put of bulb-life & wheel-work in monk & nun outtakes later released along the rim of gusto pixels making letters bloom in foot-candles at pre-tsunami highs not wanting to draw evil with too fine a point but sharpening the picture of how to soar why not ask for auto-magical for a permit to re-enter without a body without a script without counting on rain to push forthcoming up to knee-high by listening to standards or waking up to a pile of feathers & a decapitated bird art that is latent restricting jumping off a bridge unremitting reorienting seeking by descending in half steps in fifths in antecedent sketches in microtonal intervals collecting flight patterns by a light that could always pass the bottle or at least huddle on the porch of other epics a translucence that eventually dawns on the inexpert echolocating the arrangement of cuts buried in swish-pans in the third bullet of a job talk beyond fields bound for a territory not yet thought of but revealed by juxtaposition studying air intake or thirst unraveling from the spool of the world creatures in leafy margins letting their numbers be known long before migrating over guessed distances crisscrossing cerulean to boost invisible tapestry with scissors & paste crosscutting snapshots of the action against the enemy of space taking the whip to t-square to find that good smell of the fetish set fire to authority in response to the call of need inventing the names of stars not yet making the scene

cloud in the shape of a revenant

her credit may not cover
what she spent in this dwelling

> where divisions seek carriage again & again
> keeping a form for what doubling might follow

in set-widths of carefully bending her compass
which from some degrees

> are wrecks of the childhood home
> sending her wanting a profile

or one too many face-saving grains
flouncing like a sad dance

> & yielding to a strange place
> from which to observe a landscape

it's easier to blame the past
odd & even days

> siloes straying from what will become her twinning
> not giving these lyrics leeway to resist

the middle feet of the indexed
the previously fingered

> what she suspects is embrace
> what she thinks can be elation

as if in tacit fealty to tie specter to quarantine
becomes the trellis no stanza could contain

        & burns as red as summer changing frames
            claiming a raiment of graffiti

the inerasable & shiny self
bearing a binary complaint

            in a chorus to chart as difference
           among the other at each return

cloud in the shape of the rhythm method

bead work is a form of estimating home
to predict when to brandish a barrier
& when to leave *sub rosa* in the month

be sure to see the ad
that peddles hankering in the right way
by using charts & noting gaps in the disposition of a robe
      or cadence stopped when it might be strange
for a strobe light to bring you closer

there's an app to subtract eighteen   to subtract eleven
in the former style of pickling

it's said one in four kill the rabbit
      by ignoring punctuation
by not noting they *all* died
in the act of measurement

relying on fickleness that tracks texture change
      recalling that *tools do matter*
unless benders skew data
or speed the tempo of holding back

blends from the underside appear in test strips
that forecast circus moves
      or stripes of a stripper pole
seeing wingspan in a three-ring binder by the bed

this knavish dance proves caving in
ain't synched to clever bending or arithmetic
      & red tide is more a blank state
than everyone aligned with your plan

a willing writer can find middle ground with a willing reader
to picture company in yellow paired with tea
    to improve a teaching moment on motility
    to find which tempi shortcut an oocyte sighting
    by enacting vowels in the fashion of swooning
or in other words   *it's a good day to smile*

meanwhile being leery of copper
the seed wriggles for capacity
in route to   growing book clubs
        swelling bowling leagues
        filling the flat parts of church

stay baby-free is a quip
for backing to the bumper of dawn
& a trip that makes three

the word from the pull-out generation
is fill a cookie tin with rocks
put your feet in & when clattering is heard   stop

cloud in the shape of first clarinet second chair

beyond the tapered undercut of tone & ligatures in black nickel
she conjures scissortails cutting glass with a knack for shaving
grass to sought sound & pealing back sky to a soupçon of blood
ballast then all balloon she breaks with symphonic with silver
plated thread that turns pages for a system torn from the edge of
evergreens & replays episodes born to larger flight while strings
force the yes/no faith demands florescence stalls by dissolving
a smile pretending embouchure between recidivist movements
while poised to cleanse invisible she takes wind in her mouth
& eyes the maestro's hand trending one seat hence recalls a
childhood tune *in the chalumeau register* lifting from a cropland
fence with aims on the moon to carry the solo that never comes
locating the upside of withholding her breath yielding to eights
& sixes to altissimo to a score pronouncing another tiny death

cloud in the shape of just friends

enveloping as soothing is slippery as reckoning after contact for
so long admitting unease with an undercarriage breached by
defective geometry where everything is equidistant but more
or less a decorative push against functional like abacus-heeled
shoes measuring feet this surface tension in the old swing
gesture tests kinetics with a cipher wanting pleasure in the
ability to fall noting the bar set by sonny in a sky full of hawk
lingers lower on the page mixing blend with bent & pushes
back on a belt of pasturage bouncing the blue number among
stars to be outside mode changes & not modulations under
the question when does rhapsodic become a relief map cloaked
as more words on display as vistas that co-exist in rests even
if diction can't seize sadness but gives way to a wet glide path
to finding treasure in uncorrected proofs genus like genius is
a process accommodating havoc the end crawl thru glitter as
go-to in the toolkit giving viewers a glimpse behind shut bodies
in a sleight-of-hand appearing to cover its preceding beyond
what according to its service reveals the many removes to true
distilling wreckage is where no passenger is carried but rounded
by impingement to square pining with a tonic conveyed as
a dissonant bird thinking eight miles ahead & not saying it
wants to sing but swells by the puppet of its mouth in the many
mississippis between beseeching & received tintinnabulated
relics where filament exhales is a phrasal transposition when
auxiliary in twilit collapse poses contrapuntal swapping trying
to win the stepwise failures to rise above *moth & rust & thievery*
thru the trust of disbelief & assumes it's a far cry from a ringing
endorsement thermals stoked by motions burn to rush hip
to hip to reenact the stroke of nostalgia before succumbing

to diminishment thru the lens of better seeming ground
in sounding to take hold of space around traipsing seeking
whispers reaching inside all antecedent gleaming but not sealed
with a kiss

cloud in the shape of intervallic breaking
of the flow

within the spell of a short stretch of
days it is now the time of spiders or
the interstitial siren-song to minuscules
promising open space

was flap enhancing lift around an obdurate body
will be a pickup working straight out of the shrink-wrap
was a shudder in the many folds of modal sounds of any scale
will be solving tensions by modulations played sequentially
was a more stable platform for cantilevered suspension
will be choosing a minor or diminished or augmented way
was a plash laid bare by insouciant bundling
will be 2-note progressions getting mixolydian on that ass

when our elite mechanics practice
fixing to level rides their syntax is
rougher than punchlines please pass
the brown from the secret cupboard
starboard amidships casing a plastic
expanse on the sea of underneath in a
drift-step dance with your city of shiny
feet in rising labyrinthine staggering in
a way of bodies saying hello to crooked
cartwheels hiding roundhouse kicks to
think beyond a taste of tides beyond
confines *read on a sunday or two
evenings* however many nines uptime
won't take the sting out

say what again

was the clap of wings by use of a fling mechanism
will be seven natural notes sharpened or flattened
was a mushroom casting infinite thru the sense of a window
will be mockingbirds chasing crows with the semblance of jays
was phrygian metal riffing in work obeying lusters
will be a double take on the surplus taste of double soup
was the detritus the sluice produces
will be what wonder always does to skin

for Laura & Fred

cloud in the shape of an edible
inside the rothko chapel

(southwest panel)

when a guest trips past tomorrow's apples with verges firmly
drawn to find the vessel where the host is kept & eats divinity
the party goes south

(west triptych)

i lift a gummy to my mouth & every salivary swells in syrup
heralding a sly distillate trying to balance folly & weight with
the location of self in its ambiance to tell if i repeat disturbances
or declare there's nothing moral about a trolley

the paintings sell empurpled as lay recitals altered by the
strongest draft replacing something of care for inclement days
when bearings fade & pewter drops its freight to claim a sky
already dead

several schemes vie to be topmost in my head to see gradients
beyond the pledge of sizzle from a heaven stripped of pigments
crafted by that *old & evil plumage* once myth starts to fizzle

(northwest panel)

who is god get me god get me a god type get me a young god

(north apse triptych)

this bucolic circus diffused by real study is built at full scale
in the fraught value of gloom confessing a human caked in
grease & the last out of the clown car into a temple of unbelief
crowned for ecumenical conviction

thru wild onions dancing early & breathing in that made place
of new airs from old-world birds sounded by a rosined wheel
turned by *blue blue blue* asking among tonic & transcription
what reaps steel from these cold remains in the manner of
fenestrations

thru a stand of dogwood after all deciduous let fall that holds
up chocolate in high percentage & lifts spirits from an ocean of
surcease looping like ouroboros inked on the wrist of a barista
sculpting foam in botanical taxa or a kind of worship in a cup

(northeast panel)

thru the memory play of a church repast swearing *a chisel is the
most beautiful thing* casting butter beans & okra as diving in
with bated breath & trusting fingers over turbulence or a plush
lamb once you float off to your fate

(east triptych)

when doubt becomes the pentimenti of crimson working the
middle of plums or shades left nodding to byzantine is faith
edged in a harbinger of gore the transmutation of blood &
bread held firm with rabbit skin glue in the bandit tradition
that robs with clean hands & walks me thru undertone as mind
spill throbbing *tragedy ecstasy doom*

who is god get me god get me a god type get me a young god

synoptic semblance agrees even where deviancy is manifest i fancy death outside the place of ascent spun by books that don't admit a clash of codes dosage is the trope of a simulated day standing in for corruptions that creep into the text of the body or omissions that burn to trim clay selling the magic of notes left out among hard-edged limits & texas outbuilding X-ness shaking heavy cream to butter in a jar with signs of blood my blood my kin in love with admitting light bright as pindar's doves braiding redeye gravy & sun

(southeast panel)

an off-compass blade inside the elbow to the wrist opening with tuning & spilling ambrosia by framing measure in monument & elides his lids his hooks his wounds *evincing a sheen the internal lacks* & pushes back on adoring the plumbing ground

(south panel)

the last paint job is the climax of the sonnet sorting signals in bidding to abide behind three-on-the-tree not driving or naming key in the usual way & reading marrow spread by passage these lyrics rise or swoon together in praying beyond the role of redeemer lowered by tackles to keep me swallowing bliss

cloud in the shape of a western in syndication

on the backlot of wyoming
the rodeo is branded golf tees
& the sundry words for saxophone
       playing allegiance to an unburied hatchet
where itinerant ghosts exhale cake
served from the tread of a boot

where no count rigs the cowhand's bull rope
to get thrown early
       not knowing this plan won't last & will backfire
like all subterfuge from the fully shaded scoot of a shadow

there is real blood found in the broken-ring depiction of
blood
on the sacred tree with nine fronds
       there are six ways to mount a horse
one with two bullets in the back
the rest fictions of the moving target

history retreats past ruffled feathers
repeats as used condoms tossed by the hero to the vacuum
where his temper was spent
before a fish wrapped in newsprint is dropped on his stoop

he hopes this crest won't sound again
in a future that makes sense
despite flames lifting to a curtaining aesthetic
as spring tides ride the bad luck of harvest
into the perigee syzygy of

                earth   moon   sun

the barrel racer wonders how
the vernacular of her ranch might scale
beneath bruised skies over open grazing
        that echo the recital of her next move
like a bugle declaring chuck

she lusts for st. elmo's fire
on the horns of the first cut
or watusi weedy after too much black sage
& decides utterance is for those
who would seek to locate listening

long weary with second bananas
the clown stumbles past divinity
thru a yard of daffodils
        under a constellation of twenty dimes
backslides to buckaroo thinking

        you know what

                                chicken butt

        you know why

                                cow pie

cloud in the shape of a cloth over a birdcage

unknown sleeping
         sometimes known as perching
strays from a plumed range of thinking
in last cornering   stalling   gathering
         good airflow covering a cloche
to prevent dust & exterior glow
esteemed a banquet for others
                 in mouthfuls of toasted notes
waking from a starling vision
         of three descents to rise

transdermal delivery of forethought
cursive script raising discursive strew
lion   ass   hyena   snake   dragon   fire   ape
         seven the measure of spatial correlation
at the risk curve of sky
         lacustrine spilling in a tipple flute mash-up
calling all seers across murmuring

the theme of whipstitch from faraway is so tender
& a ritual of startling sparks
         & passerine vessels exhausting count
chased to collecting by threats at the edge
             more a gouge than a knife
spinning the nearest neighbor theory
tossed in scale-free correlation across meadows
mimicking bones in a labyrinth hegira

skull clocked & seeing stars is spectrum swap

in a ticking dance
        in preface to adagios
                caesura awaiting seizure
before a pulsed apparition strikes blue
splitting night into seed music
        praising likeness of light inside chambers
by celestial apprehension

cloud in the shape of the person
who wasn't coming

she answers
the dog talking backwards in a green sky
with fingers to say she's true
& stands behind refusal of story & twirls her hair

detained by a gold desk
       taken by the beauty of their instrument
that would play her
she conjures rhododendron collapse
from a flash freeze watching the picture bloom
       the exposure sink
knowing delay will count as strikes against her

she acts out invisible numbering
on the whiteboard not there
like hallowed birds chasing
on the wheel of a hollow vase
       to construct the desired figure
as they measure feet in a load of crush & run to rule her hands

she staggers tempo seeking destiny
sits on dynamited rock shaking density from her plan
what's said in sleep is gifting she collects as repair
she sees the stitching of her mirror as repair
       keeps a length of sun set on trying to catch her
reaching thru the hue of tornado weather

cloud in the shape of dice night

bowls passed clockwise
        then counter
until right-handed becomes left

unfolding smoke
exhaled over six chances on five
thrown to felt
        something near feeling
hazards scored by working sums
that grasp the acidity & alkaline of dirt
as the shaker of bones tallies

guineas rally in a cedar
roosting under the turn of constellations
we've fixed to a kind of fidelity
        from aloofness
when we glance up to the past
a doe stamps warning as her fawn burns hard eights
        unnumbered times
in seeming indivisible speed
streaking to defeat invisible clout

a cut-out of plywood
        as hanging light
names assembly
& is bigger than this cargo
all sorry for the same thing
recalling his recent fall

he would laugh in *wood church*
if he knew mechanics felled him
he should've figured

                incline   fulcrum   the toll of gravity
how seraphs roll

his smile on the wrong side of oak was a mask
or unhitched glee helping us to fathom his leaving
& re-stitch community left in a lurch

        olson said

        this morning of the small snow
        i count the blessings, the leak in the faucet
        which makes of the sink time, the drop
        of the water on water…

we are ever shoving off
to porous thresholds
to reconvene in some mineralized elsewhere
as tumblers without shores

                        in memory of Charles Murphy
                    (and the skies are not cloudy all day…)

cloud in the shape of mae west

is facing thirty-two Cs in the preamble to embracing like a
mother or bespoken whore as a different worth of hourglass &
more or less useless to delay what's coming nothing doing but
to love the curve of earth the rejoinder of sky not contrasted to
be a door & contrary to an appetite for seconds *pack in pack out*
not packed right ventures a gesture of symmetry reaching with
a dancehall move not there to pull for emergency while nylon
buffeted by gusts rapidly heats & contrary sides of the canopy
fuse removing any chance of opening when cylinders shift the
work in an absence of free operation in axial relation with offset
conditions & forces long ago arranged as predetermined cost

is when the mind splinters to fluctuating iconography now
saving twenty-two stars from bankruptcy now chemists
generating gas now a jail-break plot in profile & shape control
during flashbulbs & rolled out red carpets now *white sponge
cakes with incomparable crème coated in a fine chocolatey layer*
now drinking coke on a sofa made of lips none can shirk the
blown periphery of theatre in the round or the trees showing
wind cohering by intrusion in the same blue in a scene needing
lift but left with a lust of little B-4 inflatables keeping heads
above trouble little *diamond lil* enacting conical elements of
front grille assemblies or the sentiment of innuendo hopeful
for a little touch of hairy in the night now is the sometime to
come up and see you

cloud in the shape of a consumer diorama

start your search engines at the bubbaplex
& chart the planned obsolesce of dolls
      equating reverential space to swapping paint
on the left turn only circuit

the falling force of drift parts with the data lake
& banks on understeer ubiquity
to enlarge the appearance of true
      a predefined season projects heat
by repeating the throb of a star

rubbing outside walls plots camber
in the spread of price check language
within five traffic lights of here
& begs the question *can engines reason*

the sneaked cigarette quotient is clear
on shopping cart desertion in tracing transience
predictors so the face of an egg avatar
keeps our bliss in mind

ants line the sink
skinks slip below content scraping
in a gloss not far from rape
      the durable goods report is glanced then tossed
like a spritz of appeasing to reify trends

despite safe incandescence or the invention of gin
calipers might turn sad if the sample size returns
lagging indicators of late crepuscular light

if the fontanel quotient is soft
on how much hooch is drunk by noon
          linguistic shift won't mean conversion rates
unless restrictor plates are scrubbed
to test for instantly or soon

slot-based algorithms guess
which objects float in vanitas paintings
while peepers & other keepings
of the pulse whirr behind parataxis

proximity pay cheapen this cut-out tableau
but brooks the shimmer of yes
          like a yellow jacket
caught in the thrill of a saccharine snare
& deemed stingless as if no one was looking

footfall & voice print ape the patterns of a fencer
open the smack of tomorrow's mixed grill
by the code of absence collapsing use
before checkers flag another bad day at the track

cloud in the shape of a bunny

enjoy the coin toss
of accelerated quiet
tilting at chaste
        at sugar lifted sails
pushing a slow intaglio
of mushrooms up
in the tradition of

                    any sound
                        that cannot be heard

your slow cakewalk thru empty
doesn't stop for the best seat
or the indwelling tones
of dodecaphonic buzz

your stardust still listening

cloud in the shape of the business of
a small flying thing

airlift from holly to copse over the fire pit past the closely cropped lawn under chairs & discarded dog toy across an area *not relative to the number of objects in it* savoring the raw sensorium of voyage & the steady clip of joy composing itself *buzz passing for thought* not stopping for concepts where the validating cause might be color or volume or a prompt to note hierarchy no telling the height of fancy when wingbeat perturbs a field to excitation in brisk repeating disturbing minimal air a speck a tuft a fraction of a plume indifferent to the view of one day ceasing to be a marvelous form even against a pairwise disjoint family of sets as if no there is there delighting mainly in a state of belonging bound for who knows where some shade a leafy nap a spot for parturition open to chance deviation & the folly of gamboling by a line made up of several points of departure resisting the least of gravity to be most distant from the idea of flight & what seems like a go at mastery to best loblolly white oak sweetgum is pull up to twirl ground in a register of telescopic not seeing sequence thru an optic of tanager blue spotting leveling as circles open or shut & curve within enclosing denoting areas of overlap becoming a realm of bafflement as if that mattered flush in aleatory reveling before a swift prodigious strike

cloud in the shape of her bridal chamber

now we lay us down among murphy toothed leaves to trundle
in fields we sampled by a syncope performed in public testing
endurance choosing cushion for the falling apart years whether
in minute flowers that suddenly show beyond the garden bluets
the creamy-throated as schuyler said or in heroic verse epistle
ramped in imitation that matches our sheets retiring to dream
apart together resuming the pliable years the harvest the shared
belief in other syllables telling time by blowing thistles over
a fold of couplets taking rooms how does the neap flood of
sentiment hold confusions as favors as the interior course to
honey peeled back peering in calling for a spark as spheres
layer above fir tree days after the great fire coming together
in a hotbed flap of garments lost in cherishing the truckle of
first fragrances & trochees that taper off to muted shadows
submitting to meet in sleep

for Phoebe

cloud in the shape of range repair

a negative cosmology faults the downdraft & reduces plexus in a harpsicord manner to the best wallet photo as a picture of cash out the door mouth hewed to name us the perfect subjects of shame upsells fear by worrying the story behind how degrees are theories closing in on the area over which animals seek food & sure maybe victorian masturbation was a big deal & french horns syrup concern but we chose not to sweat papyri & the history of lust that delivered him the distance a gun can send a bullet to mend we kept distrust at arm's length instead of backing conviction but never learned as caramel sea-salt people to perform praying for convection to bring blue cones back to us on the pedestal of before

cloud in the shape of an ear in a pond

after Eva Hesse

when we touch fingers across space
a pine processionary breaks
from a shared sky
        creating a layer of wash
with wings that echo tuneful
by the way they convey wishing

troughs between waves in fluid interface
bend densities only bones can hear
by pressure sent past limits
handed down in the give it takes
to promulgate thru fluid

when cording drops in bathymetry
she elongates time
in the range of weight to depth
& warps this banked body
the way desire changes distance

while i replay yielding to shadows
        thru viscous shallows dappled
in doppelgänger cinnabar
as depending leaving painting again

cloud in the shape of dark & stormy

my safe word is *more* & a tiki bar insistence beats away from the backroom reprise where hidden is on display where line-caught valences of pudency bound for binding show signs of resistance or broken shining in white air trembling if the glamourous preset is turned off by an uncanny notion of sampling *riding it out* is the ratio of penumbra to aquatic of totem to blowfish when a future condition of six hours past *five in the afternoon* adheres to looping inside a square a blueprint addressing exotic divisions waits for honey between loosies like landlubbers enamored with chop with a corrugated sea in a complex nose of crafting the pour of grapheme synesthesia over cubes of tasting notes that raise a drink in sinking to ascend

for Jenny & Laura

cloud in the shape of the rapture
brought to you by KFC

an order of thigh
sent thru static has more sway on delight
        than eight bars of *the king & i*

tines of their sporks are best tuned to eating soup

the second shift drops a lot
to keep headcount up
as do pendants
spoofing infinity into the parking lot

telephone lines accrue a cloud a tree a lodestar
        the corner of a sign

on TV the contestant buys a vowel
        to solve *a thing*
& win a trip to orangeries

one cop car means a run on biscuits
two's responding to a false alarm from yesterday

a tree nurse yields to trumpet creeper
        & gets trouble to go
others hope for a jingoist whoosh

lower gas prices remain a tailwind
if we agree to not install malware
or launch packet floods

the fry cook takes a breather between baskets
& keeps a weather eye on wings

the postmodern colonel
in white on white on white
is all about revelations
like winning back position as the top chicken chain

        could be five for five this time
                instead of two by two

finger-licking good

cloud in the shape of a good place to eat & sleep

the cloud in my head
wide to the edge of the world

Jonathan Williams

when we close our eyes the secret work of flavor houses starts enlarging grain build & yeast migration flush rivets of the fuselage lift spirits doors are equipped with slides & i would hold you but they're overbooked & turned away standbys just know you're mine & the trip will soon fix issues shrunk to studied textures it's not certain if we'll be cherished but can certainly count on fluids or living beside that place too large not to be in the center of it all the time detecting hints of toffee & cane in the vents noting how the sweeping glass curves of the roof subsume the worry of not enough drought-tolerant fruit somehow i missed TVs unfolding & am lost as progress is retrograde for the gold rush not the way we're pointed though it seems to be the hour of arrows & engineers *do not disturb my circles* say the teeth behind soaped hands in the movie with the girl next door gazing thru a rusty screen knowing this is one of many thresholds before her hopes are dashed by the hostess job revolving a lazy-susan near blossom-carved backs & crashing into matriarchs orbiting in their bee until waves curl the other way to cancel praise & complaint we return from the theory of inside where speed is silent wishing on blistered grapes between stars before charcuterie plates rattle & rouse & landing cards are tendered to find the 6-row barley heralds sugar & the cooperage learned the best way to bend staves to urge a deeper soak line though the strain needs laddering nosing sweet mouthfeel a bridge between rounds we heed chimes & the litany of arrival conceived as thoroughfare control as revenuers seek dark trees to peddle spent grain as mystic provender to the blue horizon before the pilot puts us down

cloud in the shape of money
long as train smoke

after Velázquez

to please the court
he opens with a flourish of scrap & dispersal
                    breaking the course of projection
cast to adjacencies
            & stands as threshold
                        in a posture of folding breaths
ventriloquially asserting the exact width of now
                obeying the want of hand & eye
without stains on his sleeves   without straining
to display balance inside a locomoting range

                        a trade of gazes gives up inscapes
thru a bloodline marred by blows
drawn to the habit of etiquette
            in a pageantry beside his stretcher
his spiritual quest to record the action
of crushed ideas
decked in panniers & whiskers
apportions lower rank to a pride of place
                on a scale of embroidery
                a dog   two dwarfs   the crook
of the chamberlain's arm
            a switchyard point of vanishing

& the namesake ladies usable as angle & lift
            as avatars of a sideshow
as forms praised for waiting   with gifts
that vary from wardrobe care to lines

against the latency of psychic truth
                  offering cups   or reading posts
to who could be thought volatile in air
in the boundary of skies
                            before wedding the sun

their skill in tongues echo a sampling of doves
            in a serial clash
a discourse of whites & grays set to flight
to reach a coffined will
within a bedchamber crisis   or knot system
            bowed by corporeal disruptions
splitting lore into pianistic takes
of trembling ladders   the *infanta* caught
            in the impulse between custom & light

his theatre of boxes replots difference
by extending the grammar of paint
            talks in tablets smeared with wax
& the most kissed face in an apparitional role
is something worth curtseying to
            a value target dear to his brush
        a sovereign in his pocket
betrayed by beveling that reveals
reflection adrift in renditions of sea

call it *love of the rim of the wound*
from the view of a throne
                    mending sagittal dimensions
holding meaning back as mortals facing a god
above the countenance of *soon come*

railroads the academe in a redo of tableau
                      elides distance within a sacrificial hide
conducts the episteme as belonging bent twice
upon itself & ending in a bell   *torn voice*
sent to an order added after on his chest

                        this is a god dream

acknowledgements

thanks to hypertext transfer protocol, gertrude stein, brewster higley, street signs, bumper stickers, *las meninas,* placards, talking heads, a certain seattle dispensary, william parker, ingredient labels, woodland pattern, rachel blau duplessis, partial fortunes from cookies, brochures, copenhagen, frank o'hara, propane, michael & isabel franco, several hawks, the online etymology dictionary, beckett, joyce, closed captioning, foucault, airline safety announcements, lorca, shards of news, waiting room lit, rosie's twin kegs, the wit of friends, *edificio sayonara,* venues to sound out & flex & their lovely hosting of their curating, tony torn, the ways of magpies & songs of wood thrushes & cries of pileated woodpeckers, nathaniel mackey, nathaniel tarn, mink stoles without the minks from the ghosts of ashbery, spicer, duncan, every available grapheme, snippet, couplet, tome of beauty, song, hum, stutter in proximity, xit the bear, jalapeño raspberry jam, the new england conservatory of music, wikipedia, thomas merton, other people swimming, monograph opining, kanye west, critical studying, versioning or exactly resembling as first appearing in *hambone, black box manifold, dispatches, fluland, poetsartists, queen mob's teahouse, the new guard review, the well review,* & the readers & editors for taking in, taking care of, looking out, the whitney museum: open plan 4/21/16, john cage, words or musings or stupefying speech acts from side streets, nyc, *pulp fiction,* the department of performative studies at nyu, jackie mclean, *dark church,* london, louisville, scissor & pasting in parallel or at cross-purposing or in abject adoring, *the posthuman,* dante, *the argonauts,* j. peter moore, h.d., catch phrasing of advertising, cy twombly, chris tonelli, norman & alice finkelstein, coffee, peter o'leary, sally, minx, dave, muffin/mike, the only-ten-i see, the almost theatrical quality of highly controlled sceneries, lee ann brown, *glass, irony & god*, aldon lynn nielsen, *hello, la jolla*, so & so, backyard hens, ben lee, always, always, always phoebe, eden hall, various gnostic texts, penn state, xavier, *in the shadow of numbers*, ambient sound, the seminary coop, brett ralph, capoeira, colin mcdonald, alan golding, the chainsaw club, tyrone williams, ornette coleman, almost all of the books of the howe sisters, cecil taylor, various writers of liner notes, *samba*, excellent shots of whiskey, lee lozano, chatham county, nc, rothko, his chapel, *certain magical acts*, the occasional smoke, *the bridge*, the interstitial life between time zones, among waking & dreaming, regarding piece-work shifts, arthur jafa, *snowflake*, david antin, robert & elizabeth murphy of dos madres, curious angles of light, ruth lepson, the smell of wild onions, darcey steinke, the taste of cherokee purples, early girls, better boys, sweet 100s, dad, when dad was here, & the unfettered alabama that spills from my mother's mouth.

About the Author

KEN TAYLOR is the author of *first the trees, now this*, *dog with elizabethan collar*, and *self-portrait as joseph cornell*. He is the founder and editor of *selva oscura* press. He lives in Chicago with his wife, Phoebe and their dog, Dave.